Impact

Stories of Change Makers, Creators,
and Everyday Women
Doing Extraordinary Work

Samantha Tradelius

Impact / Samantha Tradelius — 1st ed.

Paperback ISBN: 979-8-9850057-0-7
Hardcover ISBN: 979-8-9850057-1-4

Dedication

Dedicated to the women who have inspired me

Nancy Sofie Strickler

Mother, Inspiration, Healer

Nancy Sofie Strickler is the owner of an insurance firm and a retired Registered Nurse. She is also my mother. Nance is a class act. The youngest of seven kids, she is 5 feet tall, feisty, and a bombshell beauty inside and out. My mom would work the graveyard call shifts in addition to a 36 hour week when we were young just so she could be home for my brother and I. She would always be there when we came home from school. She sometimes worked several days straight with no sleep. She never missed a softball or hockey game, she led the Brownie troop and drove us wherever life led us without a single complaint. You knew that if Nance threw on her Chanel Coco Pink lipstick that she meant business. To this day, she shows up, she never misses a call, and she can tell you how to fix, heal, or cook anything. My mother is the reason I am the woman I am today. I remember one day when I was young, we were sitting at a redlight. My mother started to tell me a story of a woman she worked with at the hospital who had suddenly lost her husband. She told me this woman didn't even know how to write a check. With tears in her eyes, my mother said, "Sami, no matter what, you always need to be able to take care of yourself." I have never forgotten these words. I owe everything that I am to my mother. Her life is a testament to hard work and commitment.

"No matter what, you always need to be able to take care of yourself."

Barbara Strickler

"GG", Witty, Biggest of Hearts

"GG" as I knew her, was a woman of many talents. She was a woman that never quit. Finding herself as a single woman with three children in the 50s, she did not have an easy life. Working three jobs many times just to feed her babies (my father, aunt, and uncle) she never quit or complained. She just kept going. The stories she would share with me as a young woman were of how important it was to put one foot in front of the other and keep going. "Life, she would say...is given to you. It's you that has to make something of it." I had an incredible relationship with her speaking weekly up until she left this earth in 2017. We spoke about everything from life's current events, personal struggles or just sometimes a good chuckle. Barbara Jean was a woman ahead of her time with fashion. Always in a pair of pumps and tailored pencil skirt. "A woman should look and feel good," she would say. GG was my inspiration in founding Sparkle Foundation. One of our last conversations we had was me sharing with her how she inspired me to do so and we both had tears in our eyes. I remember telling her I never shared her story that she was the reason with anyone because I felt that was a hard story for our family. One of the last things she said to me was, "You must share my stories Samantha, because there are so many women like me." Every day I live my life in her honor. To help women in any way I can. The biggest badass of them all, Barbara Jean.

"Life is given to you. It's you that has to make something of it."

Lynn Tallerico

Giver, Brains, Talent

Lynn is an artist, boutique handbag designer, and maker, but she wasn't always on that path. She was a Certified Public Accountant and entering midlife before she decided to switch things up with her company Lynn Tallerico Handbags. Our paths crossed when I was seeking gifts for the Sparkle Mothers with the Sparkle Foundation. She showed me around her studio while telling me about how and why she makes her handbags. I was completely enamored with her craft and mission. Lynn doesn't just make bags. Each bag is a statement that makes every woman who wears it feel uniquely special. Each of her bags is mindfully made with ethically sourced fabrics. She is giving and kind. She is the pinnacle of fearlessness, following your heart, and empowering others.

"My goal is to continue to earn a place in your closet while making this world a better place."

Rose Forbes

Focused, Risk Taker, Action Maker

Rose Forbes is the founder of Two Tree Events, an idea formed while working hard behind a bar that grew into one of LA's leading event companies, hosting some of Hollywood's finest until the Pandemic hit in 2020. While business-as-usual had come to a grinding halt, that didn't stop her. Rose, along with an amazing group of folks took the pandemic head on by taking on the task of responding to the food crisis overwhelming our major cities. Support + Feed was founded to handle this task and they have served over 65,000 meals to date between two coasts. When Rose and I were young women, we shared evening plans with each other and later in life that conversation turned to business struggles and wins. Now we nonprofit lean on one another. Rose is the ultimate example of fierceness. She loves to serve those in this world and wants nothing more than to make it a better place. Rose is a shining example of what can still be done in the most challenging of times.

"There have been times that I have taken on projects that I wasn't sure I really knew how to do when I started, but once I got going, I realized I did know how to do it after all. Taking those leaps can be tough though!! Learn to trust yourself."

Dr. Erin Bennett

Creature Lover, Dive-right-in Gal, Kitchen Dance Party Enthusiast

Dr. Erin is a veterinarian and champion mom. Erin is a dive-right-in go-getter. In her 20s, she packed her bags and moved to Ireland to study to become a veterinarian. Without knowing anyone, she boarded a plane and set out with a bag, a dream, and tons of focus. Now Erin has her own practice in one of the hardest jobs out there. While furry creatures help us all feel warm and fuzzy, sometimes the task of treating them when they are sick is not a warm and fuzzy feeling at all. Despite this, Erin still makes time to have an enormous sense of humor and to share videos of herself dancing while making dinner and finds her work very rewarding. Erin's love of animals and seeing the way in which they make people feel is what makes her tick. I have always loved her and our visits so much. In five short minutes, we can giggle, sigh, and look each other in the eye: we are birds of a feather. Erin is a boss and a shimmering light on the fact that women can do anything.

"As with everything I do I just dive right in."

Jeannie Jarnot

Giver, Supporter, Protector

Jeannie is the founder of Beauty Heroes, a company that provides clean beauty solutions to the world. What started as an idea has grown into an immensely successful business. While she has found success, she knows that it doesn't come alone. She is a true believer of supporting other women in the marketplace. Jeannie is a giver. She loves to give back and when she talks about her work her smile lights up the room. Together we have worked on countless projects with her gifting products to women across California. Jeannie is not only committed to the wellness of women and keeping them safe from unnatural products, she is also committed to ensuring that her products are safe for the earth. Through Blue Beauty, she not only ensures that her products do not harm the earth, but aims to repair and improve it. Jeannie is such an inspirational businesswoman, a maker of change, and a fellow enthusiast of all things SHE.

"I created my company for me and people like me who want and expect better."

Brandi Hutchinson
Aka Deputy Sheriff Aguilar

Giver, Public Servant, Wonder Woman

Brandi is a Deputy Sheriff and the kind of woman you want to be like when you grow up. Together Brandi and I have taken the initiative to better assist the community of Solano County. In five years we have donated hundreds of backpacks and thousands of gifts to the area. Brandi hand delivers each item to each child individually. She knows their names and shows up with backpacks, gifts, and food all on her own time and even brings her own daughters to help. Her job isn't easy and being a woman in her line of work has its struggles. Each day she awakes, suits up, and goes out to make a difference. Brandi is not just an officer of the law, she is an incredible mother, a sister, and the best friend a girl could have.

"My job is hard, especially when it comes to children. Seeing them light up when I can do something good fuels my fire."

Christina Flach

Mother, Ultimate Pretty Girl, Activist

Christina Flach is a mother, makeup guru, and a woman who has overcome some of the most head-shaking life experiences. Christina has beautified famous faces as a Masterclass makeup artist and created her own line, Pretty Girl Makeup. She does not stop. Whether it is magazines, interviews, or events she gives it her all. When Christina was faced with the sudden loss of her husband from sepsis, she chose to channel her grief into becoming an advocate for sepsis education nationally. Grief is an emotion none of us know how to deal with well. Christina however has taken her sadness and put one foot in front of the other to help others find peace in the process. Christina is a force, she is a stunning woman both inside and out. Whenever I see her, I feel full of love. To say I am in awe of her is an understatement. Christina is a living testament that focus and determination can take you anywhere.

"You don't need to prove anything to anyone."

Franza Bragg

5ft tall, Smuggler, Master Sales Guru

Franza Bragg was a woman I was introduced to as a young woman in my teens. She taught an insurance class for my parents' business LyteSpeed Learning. Little did I know at the age of 16 what an impactful woman she would become for me. She was my auntie, a mentor, and a woman who believed in me even when I didn't understand what that meant exactly. The stories she would tell me would leave my jaw on the floor. She once smuggled a parrot from Mexico in a shoebox simply because she wanted one. In the 60s, the insurance industry was made up entirely of white men, but that didn't stop her from working in the field as an eager young woman. Franza didn't give a shit about any of the things anyone said she couldn't do. She was this tiny little Jewish woman who was the definition of fierce! She outsold, out did, and stood up to each and every one of them every single day. Once she sat me down and said, "Sami, I am going to tell you something. There are four items that will get a woman out of any difficult situation and they should be kept close." To this day I keep these four items in my car at all times. Franza is missed each day and I know that she pushes me to do better every day. Women like her paved the way for women like us.

"A woman can do anything as long as she has these four items...
1) $100 bill, 2) red lipstick,
3) screw driver, 4) black panties"

Kimberly DiNapoli

Mother, Change Maker, Cheerleader of All Things She

Friendships as you grow older are more important. Those you keep in your court are the keys to your success. Kimberly DiNapoli is one of those I hold close to my heart. She is a mother, a constant-giver, and an advocate for righting injustices. So many women are subject to injustices in their careers and simply don't know what to do about it. After working in the railroad industry for more than 15 years, Kim decided that she was done being exploited, waiting around for something to change. She woke up one day and quit her job. "Nobody puts Kim in the corner." She knew that she had to be the change. Kim is the friend that will call you out of the blue to tell you how proud of you she is. She is the friend that is always there and your biggest fan. She gives motherhood, her career, and the people in her life 150% all of the time. Women like Kim are sacred and should be cherished as such.

"Standing up for you is important."

Farimah Erlandson

Beauty, Brains, Change Maker

Farimah Erlandson is wicked smart, classy, incredibly funny and knows every Tupac song by heart. When this powerhouse is not crushing it in the Court of Law, you may see her teaching law in San Francisco, volunteering at her son's school, or directing traffic as a board member of Sparkle Foundation. Farimah is one of the strongest and most tactical women I know. Being raised by powerful women has shaped her into one of the most well-spoken, driven, and fearless humans you will ever meet. From the moment she walks into a room, you know she is there. She approaches both sides of the coin in her thought-provoking banter and she does it with a dead serious face. Her ability to ask the tough questions and make the tough calls are what makes her so special. Everything she has she has earned and done so on her own. Now as a grown woman with every move she makes she makes it her duty to help other women. A mother, a do-gooder, educator, a fierce supporter of justice, and maven of life. Farimah is an example of what a powerful woman can do.

"A diva is a female version of a HUSTLER."

Beyoncé

Barbara Luhrs

Infectious Laughter, Incredible Work Ethic, Heart of Gold

Barbara Luhrs is an angel in every sense of the word. She must be one of the most giving women this world has ever seen. Barbara is a hard worker who gives every bit of herself to everything she does. Running her business L & L Property Management is just a portion of her work. She sits on the board at Sparkle Foundation Incorporated and is deeply committed to the cause by being raised by a single mother herself. She is an auntie, a sister, a friend, and fairy godmother to all around her. Barbara shows up to life every day. When she walks into a room you know she is there. She will give you a hug, tell you she loves you and dive into whatever the project is. Her laugh can be heard from a mile away, her accessories are always on point, and her vibrant blonde hair is just the beginning of this sensational woman. Barbara is the kind of person who will always tell you to keep going. Barbara is special and a woman that should be celebrated every day. Women like her are one in a million. A cheerleader, a friend, and a supporter of women everywhere.

"The first to ask about you, and the last to worry about herself."

Madelynne Mangino

Responsible, Industrious, Shining Star

Madelynne Mangino is an amazing young woman. At the age of 14, she wanted nothing more than to give her time and energy to the Sparkle Foundation. When joining the team, she made a commitment that the average young person would easily break: to be accountable, to be honest, and to be prompt. She did not disappoint. Now two years later, Maddie works alongside all of the women at the Sparkle Foundation and brings value and her young voice to each conversation. It is not often that you come across a child that is so focused, eager to take on responsibility, and to go beyond expectations. This past year, Maddie and I handed gifts to a few Sparkle Moms together. In that moment, everything became full circle and the two of us were overcome with the understanding of why we do what we do. I see much of myself as a young woman in her. She listens, absorbs, and when asked her opinion, she truly gives it. When Maddie becomes an adult, you can tell that she is going to be one to watch. Maddie is a shining star.

"Nothing can dim the light that stems from within."

Maya Angelo

Brittany Maffia

Chef, Boss, Babe

Brittany Maffia has one of the best stories of working hard and how it pays off. In 2008, she was a young woman working a day job at a local bar in San Francisco with a dream of owning a business. She worked incredibly hard to muster up the courage to quit her day job in pursuit of her dream, Urban Organics: a boutique catering firm built from scratch. Working late nights and early mornings, serving in-home dinner parties and weddings has led her to the success of landing major corporate clients and sometimes hosting 15 events in one day. Faced with the distress of the Covid-19 pandemic, Brittany was forced to adapt and reinvent herself to keep the business going and she made it happen. Brittany's story is one I love to share because she is the true tale of what a woman can accomplish. She is tough, she takes risks, she learns the hard way, and always lands on her feet with a smile on her face.

"I had no idea what I was doing, but I knew I wanted it. So I kept going."

Heather Anderson

Musician, Mother, Connector

Heather Anderson is a mother, a business owner, and a relationship builder with a zest for life and eagerness for helping others. She is the founder and CEO of The Mamahood and The Club, a set of platforms for offering support and a place to talk for women, serving over 30,000 families in the San Francisco Bay Area. Heather is a superhuman. Working tirelessly to create a community for women to connect and in doing so she has helped so many women share their struggles, stories, and to get raw. Heather works into the wee hours, night after night building this community. She is incredibly hands-on. Over the last five years, she has expanded her platforms beyond anything that she could have ever imagined, creating a safe space for women from all walks of life—a place they can all call a home base. Her most recent connective project is called The Club Concierge, a place for women entrepreneurs to share insight, grow business, and further their pursuits together. Heather's commitment to helping women become empowered is just as empowering.

"I started this because I wanted something for myself, a place for me to connect with other women going through what I was."

Kathy Kamei

Mother, Entrepreneur, Philanthropist

Kathy Kamei is an animal whisperer, creator, giver, and all around divine energy source that leaves everyone feeling lifted whenever in her presence. As a young single mother, Kathy dropped everything and moved to Bali with her two young children. Taking on the task of learning a whole new culture, Kathy never gave up hope and eventually uncovered the true meaning of life. Kathy returned to the United States years later and created a line of lifestyle jewelry specially crafted to empower and embrace women. Each piece has a mission to guide and support the woman wearing it. A zest for life and radiant joy pour from Kathy whenever she talks about why she does what she does. Knowing the impact of joy a woman feels when she wears one of her designs is what drives her forward. Kathy's story is important because it is a story of strength, growth, and finding out what fuels you to have purpose. Kathy empowers us to be the women we are meant to be.

"Women are meant to be celebrated."

Michelle Alberda

Refined, Intelligent, Compassionate

Michelle Alberda is one of San Francisco Bay Area's leading female financial planners. She has built a successful bi-coastal practice with nothing, but the will to make it happen. Michelle has made the *Forbes* lists and *San Francisco Magazine* as well as leading the top tier of production for her firm year after year. She is an author and has spoken at endless conferences sharing her encyclopedia of what it's like to make it happen when it comes to business. Michelle is a voice for women in every step she takes. She has led the Financial Women Association of San Francisco as their president and most recently created their Her Story campaign, a story of women and our journey to voting in America while raising thousands along the way for scholarships to serve young women in finance. Michelle has mentored so many young women and she is every woman's biggest cheerleader. Michelle said something to me the first night we met, "You are the chooser of the way you want to live your life. You can and will have it all. You just have to make it happen." Michelle is a champion of women helping women to succeed.

"You are the chooser of the way you want to live your life."

Dr. Karen Horton

Surgeon, Mother, Trailblazer

Dr. Karen Horton is a plastic surgeon by trade and a fellow mother. She is a micro surgeon and has a large resume of work that includes helping breast cancer patients find their way back. Her entire being is dedicated to helping women be their best selves. Karen knows exactly what to say and when to say it. Whether it's just to hold your hand after an operation or be real with expectations. Karen is the real deal. Her passion for helping women achieve goals to help them feel best in their skin is moving. I look up to her and her work so much. Karen is a wonderful role model for women everywhere.

"My role as a Plastic Surgeon is to educate, inform, and empower women."

Chanterria McGilbra

Self-Made, Philanthropist, Supporter of All Things She

Chanterria McGilbra is the founder of the Prancing Ponies Foundation, an organization that helps young women to find their worth and excel in the workplace. As a young woman Chanterria was meant for big things. A woman in STEM was not a normal thing, but it was normal for her because this woman was meant to do BIG things. Working her way up in her career she found herself with the opportunity of a lifetime to move to Monaco and get her MBA. While there she fell in love with cars and came back to the US and took her love of STEM, helping women, and fast cars and founded Prancing Ponies. She hosts an annual fundraiser and all-female car show in Pebble Beach to raise funds for her cause. Being able to help young women who were once in her shoes is a great privilege for Chanterria. Her new initiative 'Helping Women Help Themselves' helps women attend workshops and seminars that will provide them with tools to accelerate their careers and challenge the model created for women in society. She was most recently featured in the *Wall Street Journal* sporting her Ferrari 458 Spyder that she purchased herself. This car is a symbol of what a woman can do. When you see her buzzing down the street every purr of that engine is a call to all women, you can do this too!

"Set your heart on doing good. Do it over and over again and you will be filled with joy."
Buddha

Carol Wise

Educator, Dedicated, Patient

Carol Wise is a first grade teacher. She is perhaps one of the best souls I have ever come across. Carol taught my daughter first grade during the Covid-19 pandemic. During this time, I watched Carol do all that she could to keep the learning experience as normal as possible as she fought to learn and implement the remote learning template in a matter of two weeks alongside teachers all across the world. She didn't miss a beat. Just before the pandemic took hold the children were raising trout eggs as a part of a lesson and they were obsessed with watching the eggs hatch and grow. This is a lesson that Mrs. Wise would teach her students each year and each year after watching the process the children would watch the young trout be released into the wild; that wasn't going to be a possibility during this time. To make up for the children having to miss out on this opportunity, Mrs. Wise retrieved the young fish from school and recorded herself releasing them into the wild and sent it to the children to watch. She knew what a unique and important experience this was and knew she had to make it happen. Teaching children provides her with a fullness that can't be described. Mrs. Wise is a woman who in the direst of times thought so much more of others than herself. Choosing to record herself releasing the fish was something that went beyond what was expected of her and a lesson in the small things that we can all do to make a difference. Teachers like Mrs. Wise are special. Women really are amazing.

"My happy place is being with the children."

Rafelina Maglio

Community Leader, Mentor, Believer

Rafelina Maglio is one of those dynamic women who is deeply invested in women and seeing them grow. What is most special about Rafelina is her connection to the things she believes in. Her insights on subjects and connective nature are what make her so successful. Her ability to listen and focus on the areas that you are seeking value is state of the art. She quickly and deeply connects with whatever is important to you and and just as quickly offers a way to help or a person who she can lead you to. She is genuinely interested in helping people grow and watching them succeed. She is the kind of woman who just sends an email for no reason at all that says, "Yes girl." Rafelina has inspired so many. Women like Rafelina are unique in that when you are around her you feel a sense of her calm nature and her value and it comes with no strings.

"It is hard, but it is worth it and you will feel good when you complete it."

Sallie Deitz

Author, Educator, Timeless Beauty

Sallie Deitz is an author and esthetician. She is also my aunt. Her power career started as a flight attendant. Working in a high-demand service industry she learned the importance of patience. She was raised by a single mother and had to grow up fast with a world of responsibilities as a young woman. She eventually put herself through college taking on a day job at the Chanel counter and found her calling in esthetics. This career would send her across the world not only applying beauty care products, but teaching skincare techniques to women globally. She has helped guide many women along their way, earning her immense respect in the community of esthetics. Sallie is not just a beautiful person on the outside, but inside too. She cares, she loves and she listens. I have watched her in awe as I have grown. Her class and approach to life is so admirable. The way she has taken all of her life lessons and applied them to help others in her path has been a dynamic experience to watch. I always wanted to be like Sallie when I grew up. I still do. Sallie is an inspiration to women everywhere.

"All you need is faith, love, and hope."

Margarita Rymanova

Master of Beauty, Strong, Optimistic

Margarita Rymanova is the founder of La Cherie Beauty Boutique. She got her start as a medical assistant in the dermatology field. She holds degrees in Chemistry and Compound Pharmacy. Rita has taken her studies and her interest in the complexities of skin and brought it to her own business to provide a one-of-a-kind, tailored and caring experience. Rita was diagnosed with Stage IV Breast Cancer in 2018. The way she has taken on her awful circumstances and managed to see this as a dark cloud with a bright spot of light shining through is inspiring. She gets up, she goes to work, she goes about her business, she takes her medicine, and this is just another part of her life. Rita still travels, grows her business, and lives her life the way it was meant to be lived, forward. Recovering from operations, monthly tests and scans Rita just handles it, like a boss. Rita is a shining light and an example for just how strong women are.

"Well, I can be sick or I can live my life, and I choose life."

Shanti Wilson

Creator, Educator, Passion for Purpose

Shanti Wilson is a master of all things. She is a caterer, a photographer, a teacher, and a businesswoman. Shanti has offered an immense amount of help to the Sparkle Foundation. She created a program with her time to take family portraits of single mothers and their families. She then edits and prints them to give to the families for the holidays, creating a photo experience for women who otherwise would not have the opportunity to do so. The selflessness of Shanti is endless. She is one of the most generous people in the world. When Shanti's father suffered a stroke a few years ago and needed help running his business on the East Coast, she jumped in headfirst and learned how to run a successful business in an unfamiliar industry all from the opposite coast. Taking on this task was no easy feat, but for Shanti it was just another day. Her level of energy and immense heart leave an impact on all those who come across her. She is a shining star for women everywhere.

"Beauty isn't about having a pretty face. It's about having a pretty mind, a pretty heart, and pretty soul."
Grateful Dead

Stacey Fleece

Do-er, Strong, Wearer of Power Pumps

Stacey Fleece is the co-founder of a female networking group SKIRTS, former president of the Junior League of San Francisco where she remains an active member, sits on the board of the Sparkle Foundation, and has chaired countless non-profit fundraisers throughout the Bay Area. Stacey is a Certified Financial Analyst and has worked in hedge funds and finances with expertise in management, development, planning, and business mentoring. She lives a life of service and bettering the lives of women around her. She is an undercover badass. Her badass expertise has helped her close countless deals, gain the attention of the press, and allowed her to speak and coach groups of women about their finances. Stacey has done all of this as a single mother raising two children alone. She never complains, she just does. She is the first one to dive deep and ask the real questions; the first one to help when needed. More often than not, when I find myself in a difficult situation, I ask myself, "What would Stacey do?" Stacey would put on a pair of power pump heels and take on the day. She is the kind of woman young women aspire to be when they grow up.

"When life throws you lemons, juice them, and add ice."

Who am I

Who am I? To begin I am a woman and that is an underlined, BOLD statement. Mother to two crazy girls ages eight and ten, and married to a Gemini. Life is full to put it mildly.

I have lived my life to serve others, but not in an, "Oh this makes me look good kind of way." Instead in an, "Oh this feels good way." Empathy and sympathy are two of my greatest strengths. You always know where you stand with me good, bad, and ugly. As loyal as they come, your biggest cheerleader and if I call you a friend I mean it. Supporting and lifting women is my jam. I love more than anything seeing a woman find her passion and succeed. I also love when she finds a challenge and overcomes it.

My superpower is energy.

I have an abundance of it...always have. When I was young I was told I was a bit TOO much. As an adult it is called being "fast paced." Whatever you like to call it, I get it done.

My Why

Women are special and unless you have a huge platform, are rich and famous, or have been through some trauma more often than not, your story goes unheard.

Women everyday are doing amazing things and inspiring us all the time. This book is the stories of women in my life that have made me the woman I am today. For I am only the woman I am now because of the wonderful women who have inspired me to do so.

The little stories of these ladies and little quips have pulled me through many points in my 40 years.

About the Author

Samantha Tradelius is the founder of Sparkle Foundation, a non-profit with the intent to lend support to single mothers and their children. She hosts the weekly podcast InspiHER'd, curates the monthly S.List that features women-owned brands, and the Quarterly S. Experience geared toward bringing women together supporting local women in business. She wears four-inch heels every single day, does five pilates sessions a week, and survives on coffee and the "F" word.

She resides and works in the San Francisco area with her husband, two daughters, and two pugs.

CPSIA information can be obtained
at www.ICGtesting.com
Printed in the USA
LVHW071618201021
700976LV00006B/227

9 798985 005714